The New
SPELL~WELL

G000127553

Book 5

C J Ridout

NELSON

Contents

Thomas Nelson and Sons Ltd
Nelson House Mayfield Road
Walton-on-Thames Surrey KT12 5PL UK

© Thomas Nelson and Sons Ltd 1992
First published by Blackie & Son Ltd 1979

This edition published by Thomas Nelson and Sons Ltd 1993

I(T)P Thomas Nelson is an International
Thomson Publishing Company

I(T)P is used under licence

ISBN 0-17-424072-4
NPN 9 8 7 6

Printed in Croatia

How to be a good speller

1 Look at each word knowing that you will have to write it later without help.
2 Say each word clearly and pronounce it correctly. Sometimes we are careless in the way we say words and this makes spelling more difficult.
3 Be clear about the meaning or meanings of each word so that you can use it to make an interesting sentence.
4 As you say the word look at each part so that you know the difficulties.
5 Close your eyes and trace the word with your finger. Check that you traced it correctly then do it a few more times so that you will *never* forget.
6 Keep an alphabetically arranged word book and *neatly* note down all the words you have learned.
7 Learn the words *you* use! When writing a story, use your dictionary to help you spell words you do not know. Learn these words in the same way as you learn the words in this book. Remember to add these words to your word book! *A good speller is someone who knows how to spell the words* he *uses in his writing.*

Guidelines for writing

When writing a composition you must plan how you will present your work. The following approach will help you.

Think of all the ideas you can about the subject.
Now plan:

A beginning: How you will provide a background for your story. You must set the scene and arouse the interest and curiosity of your reader.

A middle: How the main points in the story will be arranged so that they are presented in proper order. Consider how you will bring the story to life for your reader. You may do this by thoughtful description. Think of things you would:

    see   hear   touch   smell

Describe these in such a way that your reader can share your experiences.

Try to make your reader feel the things you feel.

An end: How you will round off the story and maintain interest to the last sentence.

Think of different ways you can present your work. For example you may choose to write:

a story   a description   a poem
a letter   a report   a play

Sometimes it is interesting to write about the same topic in different ways.

1	2	3
cell	guide	skill
cycle	guilt	skilful
city	guess	fill
circle	guest	fulfil

4	5	6
magic	telegram	rely
picnic	television	reliable
traffic	telegraph	desire
terrific	telescope	desirable

7	8	9
addition	shield	permit
position	field	permission
competition	mischievous	admit
definition	pierce	admission

10	11	12
stern	rescue	width
lantern	pursue	breadth
pattern	avenue	growth
modern	tissue	breath

Stand and deliver!

highwayman
horseman
pistol
sword
rapier
jewellery
jewels
possessions
diamond
sapphire
locket
mail
booty
carriage
passenger
destination
milestone
posthouse
cloak
tricorn hat
disguise

masked
lonely
notorious
infamous
nervous
jubilant
angry
dejected
furious
valuable
heavy
muffled
restive
clattering
sinister
rutted

alighted
ordered
aimed
whipped

spurred
gathered
collected
threatened
mounted
commanded
yelled
shouted
fainted
challenged
lurked
swayed
lurched
galloped
reared

cautiously
beyond
suspiciously
dangerously
unexpectedly

Phrases

offered a reward
in hot pursuit
mortally wounded
windswept heath
wealthy merchant
lying in wait

vanished into the night
grasped the reins
band of rogues
a sharp report
treasured possessions
Your money or your life!

7

1	2	3
chance	prevent	single
balance	violent	muscle
entrance	ornament	puzzle
trance	urgent	struggle

4	5	6
area	presence	general
idea	sentence	generally
ideal	preference	gradual
seal	difference	gradually

7	8	9
autumn	spoil	select
column	avoid	selection
solemn	choice	connect
condemn	poison	connection

10	11	12
operate	excuse	enough
operation	except	rough
separate	exceed	bought
separation	excess	brought

Moving house

possessions
belongings
articles
contents
furniture
settee
sideboard
piano
television
lampshade
picture
ornament
wardrobe
mirror
crockery
refrigerator
cooker
saucepan
bicycle
removal van
address
neighbour

destination
street
avenue
assistance
farewell
exclamation
weight

valuable
fragile
precious
personal
heavy
cumbersome
awkward
household
bare
empty
friendly

packed
boxed

wrapped
tied
protected
moved
mislaid
carried
loaded
dismantled
removed
shattered
clattered
guided
exhausted
relieved
arrived

quickly
clumsily
carefully
gradually
carelessly
eventually

Phrases

assorted packing cases
a last look around
strange empty rooms
a mysterious bundle
a horrible crunch

echoing footsteps
stuck in the doorway
handle with care
an odd assortment
packed in straw

1	**2**	**3**
create	explain	bury
creation	exercise	buried
decorate	experience	ready
decoration	expect	readiness

4	**5**	**6**
explore	despair	suggest
extremely	deny	suggestion
expensive	decide	direct
experiment	despise	direction

7	**8**	**9**
accuse	again	capable
accusation	against	miserable
celebrate	straight	valuable
celebration	acquaint	comfortable

10	**11**	**12**
amuse	enormous	degree
amusement	numerous	proceed
abuse	tremendous	agreement
refuse	suspicious	screen

Pollution

fumes
grime
soot
smoke
oil
silt
sewage
plastic
containers
rubbish
waste
sludge
smog
seagull
cormorant
puffin
feathers
creatures
chimney
factory
chemical

tanker
spillage
slick
detergent
beach

unhealthy
destructive
suffering
poisonous
smoky
helpless
greasy
matted
inflammable
vulnerable
frightened
terrified
dying
noisy
deadly

toxic
indestructable
thoughtless
careless
accidental

rescue
collect
disperse
protect
spoil
starve
prevent
warn
prohibit
allow
injure
destroy
remove
improve
legislate

Phrases

selective weedkillers
open-cast mining
picturesque countryside
polluted rivers
urban motorways
radioactive waste

restocked rivers
screaming jets
stagnant pools
electricity pylons
laid waste
belching chimneys

1	**2**	**3**
favour	site	shoulder
favourite	granite	mount
glamour	opposite	poultry
rumour	definite	mould

4	**5**	**6**
marvellous	assume	glance
prosperous	assure	stance
jealous	associate	fragrance
generous	assess	attendance

7	**8**	**9**
vacant	angle	usual
elegant	bangle	unusual
ignorant	tangle	known
extravagant	triangle	unknown

10	**11**	**12**
neighbour	fashion	carry
either	cushion	carriage
neither	religion	marry
eighth	edition	marriage

Nightmare!

supper	terrible	terrified
cheese	sinking	surrounded
monster	ghostly	followed
cavern	shadowy	buried
stairs	creeping	pursued
sleep	drowsy	crouched
dream	sinister	chased
pillow	trembling	tumbled
shadow	shivering	wrestled
escape	frightened	grasped
footstep	desperate	climbed
figure	savage	forced
gate	snarling	retreated
window	fierce	haunted
curtain	quaking	described
picture	suffocating	horrified
ghost	restless	approached
gust	exhausted	
silence	choking	regularly
echo	vivid	seldom
struggle	wicked	occasionally

Phrases

thrashing about
clutching hands
falling through space
shadowy figures
horror film
panic-stricken

terrifying experiences
remember distinctly
close at my heels
familiar surroundings
someone screamed
shaken awake

1	**2**	**3**
care	capture	occasion
careful	overture	occasionally
careless	nature	occupy
carefully	picture	occupation

4	**5**	**6**
purse	succeed	guard
pursuit	success	guardian
purpose	successful	persuade
purple	unsuccessful	persuasion

7	**8**	**9**
benefit	station	tight
beneficial	stationary	loose
benevolent	stationer	noisy
benefactor	stationery	quiet

10	**11**	**12**
tomorrow	special	shoes
tonight	especially	use
together	official	news
altogether	officially	ewes

Fishing

species
mackerel
perch
trout
salmon
lobster
crab
shrimp
minnow
starfish
jellyfish
dogfish
creel
line
rod
reel
bait
fly
pier
harbour
gill

fin
pincer
scale
seagull
forecast
weather
gunwale
catch
licence
lure
float
bite

patient
impatient
rough
lonely
enormous
tiny
seasick
soaked

skilful
lucky
shiny
wriggling
silvery
tasty
beautiful
menacing
darting
leaping
splashing

wade
cast
pull
secure
exaggerate
moor
enjoy
overbalance
slither

Phrases

an enjoyable hobby
stretch of water
an old bucket
outboard motor
returning to spawn
tugging on the line

bait the hook
brightly coloured
running sideways
overcast skies
a delicious meal
river in spate

1	2	3
cover	assist	examine
discover	assistance	examination
recover	resist	imagine
discovery	resistance	imagination

4	5	6
weather	social	qualify
wealthy	racial	quantity
instead	facial	quality
steal	artificial	quarter

7	8	9
mysterious	greedy	dense
precious	freedom	intense
conscious	engineer	expense
unconscious	career	immense

10	11	12
suitable	chose	war
reasonable	choose	peace
favourable	lose	smooth
improbable	loose	coarse

Snowbound

forecast
conditions
blizzard
gale
sleet
hail
fuel
helicopter
telephone
cable
livestock
marker
flare
bonfire
signal
snow-plough
icicles
silence
stillness
radio
television

fodder
supplies
survivor
crystals
patterns

remote
buried
enveloped
starving
desperate
frosty
sparkling
crisp
helpless
glistening
crunching
starving
keen
severe
essential

lose
search
discover
freeze
thaw
flood
vanish
disappear
communicate
contact
direct
rescue
experience
describe
recount

speedily
suddenly
urgently
distinctly
unexpectedly

Phrases

completely cut off
flurries of snow
frozen waste
featureless landscape
power lines broken
Arctic conditions

leaden skies
plight of the animals
emergency provisions
foraging creatures
survived miraculously
shivering with cold

1	**2**	**3**
seize	arrange	state
receive	arrangement	statement
receipt	advertise	excite
deceive	advertisement	excitement

4	**5**	**6**
fruit	ancient	extreme
suit	grief	explode
distinguish	soldier	exaggerate
disguise	patient	expel

7	**8**	**9**
obedient	caution	score
obedience	cautious	chore
evident	ambition	therefore
evidence	ambitious	folklore

10	**11**	**12**
move	delicious	message
movement	defeat	messenger
manage	delicate	passage
management	defy	passenger

A journey into space

gantry
rocket
fuel
astronaut
destination
galaxy
zero
orbit
crater
oxygen
cylinder
universe
Jupiter
Saturn
Mars
Uranus
Earth
Pluto
Mercury
Venus
planet
computer

display
console
device
provisions
capsule
atmosphere
stratosphere
antennae
course
void
apparatus
screen
experience
explosion
space-suit

famous
dangerous
unknown
skilled
specialized
protective

expensive
complicated
courageous
timeless

zoomed
flashed
accelerated
travelled
moved
ejected
recorded
spun
revolved
boosted
floated
photographed
appeared

beyond
silently
effortlessly

Phrases

heavenly bodies
mission control
in radio contact
a walk in space
solar system

unearthly silence
successful docking
feeling of weightlessness
splashed down safely
pull of gravity

1	2	3
pave	centre	building
pavement	central	recruit
discourage	circle	juice
discouragement	circular	nuisance

4	5	6
cease	graph	complain
increase	nephew	complaint
release	photograph	fail
decrease	telephone	failure

7	8	9
difficult	necessary	imitate
difficulty	unnecessary	imitation
different	fortunate	hesitate
differently	unfortunate	hesitation

10	11	12
protect	investigate	reflect
protection	investigation	reflection
exclaim	calculate	collect
exclamation	calculation	collection

Should children watch television?

programme	sport	varied
channel	fault	amusing
character	villain	interesting
actor	thriller	musical
actress	advertisement	popular
episode	interruption	favourite
colour	control	talented
hero	contrast	skilful
heroine	volume	brilliant
producer	switch	
comedy	aerial	serialized
comedian	repeat	rationed
cartoon		introduced
orchestra	dramatic	described
image	educational	viewed
scenery	entertaining	enthralled
satellite	instructive	repeated
news	scientific	repaired
script	historical	
artist	documentary	impatiently
quiz	visual	regretfully
dilemma	political	simultaneously

Phrases

school broadcasts
a horror film
the weather forecast
cartoon time
recorded highlights

feature film
action replay
frightened to watch
glued to the screen
slow motion

1	**2**	**3**
afraid	junction	pylon
mountain	relation	rhyme
certain	population	typewriter
faithfully	section	tyre

4	**5**	**6**
destroy	daffodil	pension
design	paraffin	division
desert	suffer	vision
desperate	giraffe	confusion

7	**8**	**9**
people	sincere	accurate
terrible	sincerely	accurately
bottle	immediate	separate
jumble	immediately	separately

10	**11**	**12**
grateful	armour	remarkable
thankful	colour	believable
colourful	honour	probable
dreadful	harbour	liable

Wild creatures of our countryside

animal
bird
reptile
snake
owl
insect
badger
rabbit
otter
fox
vixen
deer
stag
mouse
squirrel
adder
swan
goose
dragonfly
warren
undergrowth
burrow

holt
lair
drey
farmer
gamekeeper
poultry
antler
venison
herd
footprint
appearance
diet
brush
scent
lichen
mountain
heather
hide

vegetarian
carnivorous
bedraggled

daring
cunning
sly
hungry
native
dangerous
graceful
nimble
agile
inquisitive
nocturnal

camouflage
hibernate
search
bound
scurry
forage
disappear
observe
glide
rustle

Phrases

approach stealthily
blood sports
natural habitat
distinctive marking
a rare species

flash of white
huntsman's horn
a loud screech
gliding silently
pathetic sight

1	2	3
length	because	descend
lengthen	applause	descent
strength	automatic	describe
strengthen	audience	description

4	5	6
supply	curious	scene
satisfy	furious	scenery
magnify	previous	scientist
multiply	serious	scissors

7	8	9
amount	condition	current
announce	expedition	frequent
pronounce	petition	accident
council	repetition	compliment

10	11	12
accompany	national	absent
accomplish	regional	absence
accustom	intentional	absolute
accept	exceptional	absorb

A derelict building

warehouse
mansion
castle
cinema
theatre
neighbourhood
cobwebs
debris
mildew
litter
rubbish
ceiling
tile
chimney
basement
spider
mouse
beetle
occupant
site
slogan
vandal

empty
crumbling
rotten
dangerous
creeking
rusty
faded
grimy
gaping
worn
dank
musty
unfrequented
overgrown
mossy
cracked
boarded
barred
draughty
condemned
eerie
ghostly

ancient
unkempt
untidy
lonely
sighing
neglected

demolished
sheltered
inhabited
broken
ruined
supported
destroyed
deserted

thoughtlessly
slowly
silently
noiselessly
steadily
unfortunately

Phrases

high-rise flats
old and dilapidated
razed to the ground
wrought-iron railings
multi-storey car park

danger—keep out
a collapsed staircase
sagging hinges
leaking gutters
a relic of the past

1	**2**	**3**
double	conquer	attack
trouble	conceal	attempt
country	consist	attractive
couple	container	attire

4	**5**	**6**
possible	lazy	determine
impossible	laziness	determination
visible	happy	confident
invisible	happiness	confidence

7	**8**	**9**
kingdom	beautiful	somewhere
seldom	plentiful	someone
wisdom	pitiful	something
dominion	graceful	sometimes

10	**11**	**12**
disappear	acid	tongue
disappearance	acute	throat
disappoint	ache	stomach
disappointment	active	heart

A visit to a big store

entrance
exit
fire door
escalator
elevator
customer
assistant
manager
cashier
department
restaurant
waitress
cafeteria
menu
refreshments
cloakroom
accounts
hairdresser
delicatessen
overcoat
suit
trousers

blazer
display
umbrella
anorak
jewellery
perfume
handkerchief
furniture
hardware
stationery
crockery
dresses
shoes
sandals
television
radio
camera
bicycle
parcel
money
cheque
sale

expensive
cheap
attractive
beautiful
stylish
colourful
bright
crowded
busy
valuable
suitable
reasonable
sensible
excellent
efficient
helpful
pleasant
polite

purchase
measure
exchange

Phrases

thieves will be prosecuted
a store detective
queues of customers
discontinued line
three-piece suite

bargain basement
latest fashions
changing rooms
10% discount
do-it-yourself

1	2	3
conquer	piano	reveal
conceal	potato	zeal
consist	tomato	search
container	zero	steady

4	5	6
mayor	daughter	waist
major	laughter	against
minor	slaughter	aircraft
motor	draught	curtain

7	8	9
rogue	rot	factory
league	rotten	horror
plague	forgot	visitor
vague	forgotten	conqueror

10	11	12
beneath	circuit	ordinary
repeat	cruise	origin
weary	guide	orchestra
hearth	acquit	ordeal

Help! Someone's drowning

scene
sunshine
river
reservoir
harbour
pier
cave
boat
yacht
crevice
ripples
fathom
meadow
waterfall
bridge
reeds
tide
rocks
swimmer
bather
situation
clothes

assistance
voice
passer-by
frogman
ambulance
rescuer
occurrence
accident
distance
exclamation
survival
condition

dreadful
resourceful
exhausted
entangled
peaceful
strong
brave
courageous
capsized

shout
wave
scream
reach
throw
row
save
rescue
struggle
carry
wrap
grope
snatch
panic

tragically
desperately
frantically
suddenly
dangerously
cautiously
successfully

Phrases

overhanging ledge
artificial respiration
picnicking by the river
dangerous currents
ear-piercing scream

lean too far
a near tragedy
kiss of life
a sudden gust
pale and shaken

1	**2**	**3**
knob	savage	explode
kneel	sewage	explosion
knead	vicarage	extend
knuckle	garage	extension

4	**5**	**6**
independent	blood	proud
indicate	soothe	journey
individual	brooch	cough
inferior	wool	dough

7	**8**	**9**
sour	prey	toast
flavour	obey	boast
vapour	convey	roast
route	survey	hoard

10	**11**	**12**
history	Arctic	neon
memory	topic	pigeon
inventory	tropic	surgeon
dormitory	cubic	truncheon

A newspaper

editor
article
column
advertisement
reporter
printer
page
copy
edition
cartoon
photograph
programme
type
news
sport
fashion
views
event
letter
description
result

headline
account
crossword
entertainment
accident
telephone
typewriter
obituary
column
announcement
capital
competition
comment

principal
foreign
local
national
topical
daily
weekly

famous
valuable
honest
accurate
interesting
exciting
favourite

interview
introduce
describe
distribute
mention
illustrate
contact
dispatch

quickly
accurately
hurriedly
punctually

Phrases

stop-press
comic strip
colour supplement
lost and found
centre spread
sports page

hot from the press
items of interest
articles for sale
dramatic headline
letter to the editor
radio and television times

1	2	3
address	nourish	diamond
balloon	flourish	diameter
coffee	journal	diary
woollen	mound	diagram

4	5	6
silent	violence	salute
silence	circumference	execute
refer	existence	dispute
reference	innocence	flute

7	8	9
several	illustrate	quarrelsome
material	regulate	handkerchief
final	emigrate	wheelbarrow
mortal	immigrate	cupboard

10	11	12
similar	argue	figure
peculiar	continue	furniture
particular	catalogue	future
calendar	fatigue	temperature

School

teacher
classroom
gymnasium
library
staffroom
dining hall
cloakroom
toilet
assembly
subject
lesson
secretary
headmaster
nurse
auxiliary
janitor
caretaker
cleaner
primary
secondary
Geography
Nature Study

Mathematics
History
English
Science
pencil
exercise
television
tape-recorder
apparatus
blackboard
picture
atlas
textbook
playground
entrance
bicycle shed
heating
uniform
corridor
blazer
cricket
netball

football
animals
punishment
rule
excursion
building

strict
modern
junior
senior
favourite
interesting
crowded
noisy

teach
learn
enjoy
study
recite
compete

Phrases

open-plan school
school broadcasts
piles of homework
fire practice
summer holidays

parents' day
Christmas concert
sports day
Physical Education
beginning of term

1	2	3
rhubarb	whistle	ocean
rhythm	whistled	pleasant
rhyme	listen	theatre
rhombus	listened	health

4	5	6
qualify	private	government
quality	climate	parliament
quarter	appreciate	argument
quadruped	commemorate	judgment

7	8	9
curiosity	luxury	wrinkle
university	luxurious	wrestle
opportunity	anxious	wrist
scarcity	anxiety	wring

10	11	12
occurred	corporal	obstacle
preferred	sergeant	spectacle
permitted	captain	miracle
committed	lieutenant	manacle

Leisure centre

squash
badminton
archery
court
rink
pool
gymnasium
sauna
equipment
racket
towel
costume
leotard
plimsolls
shower
cinema
theatre
restaurant
snack bar
refreshments

attendants
spectators
queue
season ticket
entrance fee
entrance
exit
notice board
regulations
advertisements
deposit
key
tuition
competition

enthusiastic
healthy
keen
skilful
amateur

experienced
intermediate
advanced
expert

coach
hire
instruct
teach
encourage
participate
wobble
control

energetically
nervously
excitedly
dangerously
confidently
successfully

Phrases

practises frequently
parties of children
information kiosk
keep-fit classes
air-conditioning
a steamy atmosphere
safety precautions

beginners' class
a magnificent stroke
the main concourse
professional instructor
background music
light and airy
membership card

1	2	3
damage	mineral	honesty
village	musical	wretched
average	natural	knowledge
advantage	criminal	listener

4	5	6
engine	interest	convenient
machine	interior	convenience
refine	interrupt	intelligent
decline	interfere	intelligence

7	8	9
earnest	encourage	glorious
earthquake	course	industrious
breakfast	labour	gracious
meant	plough	victorious

10	11	12
maintain	compel	accept
retain	compelled	attempt
remainder	travel	temptation
ascertain	travelled	prompt

Travel through the centuries

pedlar	vessel	uncomfortable
pack-horse	schooner	dangerous
saddle	steamer	primitive
reins	yacht	ancient
wheel	liner	modern
carriage	aeroplane	weary
cart	helicopter	reliable
coach	monorail	punctual
sedan chair	hovercraft	expensive
wagon	turnpike	muddy
galleon	toll	
engine	ford	invented
steam	bridge	constructed
railway	motorway	designed
petrol	pirate	built
bicycle	highwaymen	discovered
tricycle	breakdown	manufactured
tyre	invention	
puncture	progress	successfully
diesel	ferry	conveniently
airship	passenger	safely
luggage	fare	gradually

Phrases

a penny-farthing	rutted, twisting tracks
tarmacadam roads	public transport
space capsule	hazardous journey
laden pack-horses	a horseless carriage
journey to the moon	travel in luxury

1	2	3
committee	interval	aeroplane
possession	intersect	aerobatics
commission	intervene	aerial
accommodation	intersperse	aerosol

4	5	6
irritate	constable	propeller
irritable	detective	helicopter
irresponsible	inspector	character
irrigate	superintendent	commuter

7	8	9
parallel	noun	incline
pillar	pronoun	include
jeweller	adverb	incident
jewellery	adjective	income

10	11	12
city	essential	extract
peculiarity	perennial	extraction
reliability	memorial	exert
tenacity	biennial	exertion

Man's best friend—the dog

alsatian
collie
St Bernard
spaniel
labrador
poodle
terrier
mongrel
guide
harness
collar
lead
companion
criminal
circus
kennel
licence
owner
trick
property
pedigree

valuable
ferocious
attentive
obedient
faithful
blind
strong
wise
intelligent
amusing
playful
patient
affectionate
docile

yawn
pant
growl
snarl
whine
spring

defend
attack
bite
pounce
surprise
leap
search
sniff
guard
nuzzle
secure
fetch
carry
train
teach
team

warily
angrily
wearily
immediately

Phrases

alert and attentive
tail between its legs
anxious to please
gnawed a bone
smooth, sleek coat
come to heel

barking furiously
lolling tongue
beware of the dog
cold, wet nose
whining piteously
high-pitched whistle

1	2	3
though	anguish	usually
through	extinguish	equally
thorough	genuine	language
thought	equipment	continual

4	5	6
thoughtful	irregular	legal
throughout	interruption	vertical
thoroughly	surround	horizontal
although	surrounding	physical

7	8	9
triumph	courageous	poisonous
prophet	miscellaneous	anonymous
paragraph	hideous	deciduous
phantom	gaseous	miraculous

10	11	12
salary	recollect	equip
secretary	recognize	biscuit
military	recover	enquire
supplementary	reckon	enquiry

Rescued by helicopter

signal
wreckage
survivor
wave
radio
oasis
jungle
vegetation
palm
fuselage
cliff
island
avalanche
accident
illness
disaster
flood
stretcher
pilot
navigator
observer
searchlight

journey
countryside
surroundings
desert
engine

shivering
spotted
distressed
numb
tropical
uninhabited
sheltered
strange
foreign
terrified
frightened
fierce
loud
deafening
windswept
frozen

soaked
parched
hazardous
isolated
friendly
protective
grateful
doubtful
visible
desperate

rotated
marooned
warned
hovered
lowered
raised

gradually
accurately
unfortunately
promptly

Phrases

mountain rescue team
a crash landing
huddled together
the spinning rotor
the incoming tide

dangling in mid-air
fierce, scorching sun
a welcome sight
raised by winch
an empty silence

1	**2**	**3**
apparent	breath	grammar
appetite	breathe	beggar
appeal	cloth	hangar
approve	clothes	popular

4	**5**	**6**
approach	channel	police
broadcast	annual	practice
cocoa	announce	device
boast	funny	precipice

7	**8**	**9**
puncture	contestant	religious
adventure	abundant	tedious
stature	restaurant	various
manufacture	redundant	nutritious

10	**11**	**12**
aunt	transfer	gnaw
auction	transport	gnash
authority	transmit	gnome
autograph	translate	gnat

Robert the robot

automaton
duties
computer
breakdown
engineer
havoc
gadget
accessory
movement
motor
whirr
current
assembly
component
switch
power
strength
system
invention
science
future

leisure
fault
factory
laboratory
scientist
direction
instruction

reliable
mechanical
crazy
jointed
flexible
adjustable
untiring
inexhaustible
skilful
minute
nimble
mobile
automatic

artificial
electric
complicated
intelligent
successful
separate

assemble
weld
solder
regulate
replace
perform
function
respond
propel
guard

gradually
powerfully
independently

Phrases

loose connection
silicon chip
monotonous tasks
moving antennae
out of control
almost human

highly polished metal
battery operated
complicated apparatus
household chores
unquestioning obedience
conquer the world

1	**2**	**3**
mechanical	happened	consult
original	appeared	constant
personal	frightened	confine
historical	arrived	confiscate

4	**5**	**6**
perpendicular	replied	borrowed
vinegar	denied	produced
scholar	cried	plunged
nuclear	tied	surrendered

7	**8**	**9**
forehead	leisure	bachelor
forecast	reindeer	equator
foreground	reign	refrigerator
foresight	foreign	transistor

10	**11**	**12**
confess	stretcher	author
concern	dispatch	sailor
confuse	kitchen	doctor
confer	Dutch	supervisor

A building site

architect
plans
workmen
foreman
plumber
slater
bricklayer
glazier
joiner
electrician
bulldozer
scaffolding
ladder
drain
timber
rafter
cement
plasterboard
chimney
ceiling
bungalow

office
shovel
trowel
hammer
barrow
helmet
tarpaulin
fireplace
radiator
eaves
gutter
paint
emulsion
fence
design
kitchen
staircase
loft
foundations
trench
puddle

modern
accurate
attractive
expensive
muddy
untidy
noisy
dangerous
different
stationary
unfinished

measure
build
load
stack
assemble
advertise
occupy
climb
position

Phrases

workmen's hut
mounds of top-soil
semi-detached house
"For sale" notice
showhouse
clatter of machinery

pneumatic drill
desirable residence
double-glazed windows
a mobile crane
reinforced concrete
lorries turning

1	2	3
choir	total	attend
chorus	arrival	attention
character	criminal	attract
chemist	fatal	attraction

4	5	6
chief	inhabit	extra
efficient	prohibit	express
sufficient	exhibit	expand
science	exhibition	expense

7	8	9
agree	value	ankle
agreeable	queue	jungle
disagree	issue	title
disagreeable	revue	little

10	11	12
trio	humour	thief
tricycle	behaviour	brief
triangle	endeavour	belief
tripod	valour	believe

Visit to a castle

ramparts
moat
drawbridge
portcullis
battlements
tower
keep
dungeon
well
bailey
storehouse
gate-house
courtyard
chapel
guardroom
gallery
closet
apartment
kitchen
sundial
cellar
garrison

knight
armour
cannon
peasant
soldier
sword
catapult
helmet
visor
shield
violence
stable
sentry
torch
fireplace
gargoyle
fortress
century
tapestry
guide
admission
arrow

draughty
smoky
impregnable
historic
ancient
principal
imposing
impressive
victorious
peaceful
solid

scaled
attacked
defended
besieged
starved
surrendered
imprisoned
occupied
withstood
surrounded

Phrases

spiral staircase
curtain wall
coat of arms
commanding position
rousing battle cries

studded oak doors
vaulted ceiling
battering ram
narrow winding path
a jousting tournament

Difficult words

1

personal
personnel
recommend
restaurant

2

camouflage
licence
adhesive
nylon

3

vehicle
Terylene
memorandum
subscription

4

physician
surgeon
cemetery
temperature

5

advertisement
inoculation
antique
courteous

6

separation
symmetrical
acquaintance
solicitor

7

benefit
benefited
astronaut
anonymous

8

optician
satellite
anorak
accessory

9

cheque
prescription
protein
diesel

10

computer
tonsilitis
headache
conscientious

11

dissolve
miscellaneous
sincerely
curtain

12

yacht
amateur
professional
hygiene

A cricket match

bowler
batsman
fielder
innings
pavilion
score-board
opponent
achievement
disaster
victory
accuracy
no-ball
bails
umpire
pitch
boundary
wickets
crease
captain
interval

applause
spectators
excitement
catastrophe
attendance
contest
weather
light

attentive
cautious
additional
confident
entertain
fortunate
memorable
spectacular
straight
successful
winning

steady
nervous
thrilling
tense
hopeful
accurate
valuable

cheer
appeal
support
declare
dismiss
defeat
collapse
resume
congratulate
applaud
strike
catch

Phrases

cricket enthusiasts
exceptionally strong
fearless hitting
maiden over
skilful play
a desperate effort
scored a century

an unhappy moment
the winning stroke
to decide the issue
well-deserved victory
close of play
fielded the ball
clean bowled

More difficult words

1

business
electric
goodbye
independence

2

programme
illness
sandwich
jewellery

3

lightning
medicine
silhouette
vegetable

4

interested
secondary
mountainous
gaol

5

boundary
machinery
tobacco
liquid

6

practice
practise
question
museum

7

traveller
production
chaos
dictionary

8

concise
especially
engineer
mechanic

9

teaspoonful
reckon
system
systematic

10

parliament
government
colonel
calendar

11

therefore
catastrophe
queue
certificate

12

necessary
privilege
cocoa
oblige

Dining out

restaurant
cafeteria
hotel
waiter
waitress
menu
cutlery
crockery
glasses
condiments
vase
flowers
kitchen
chef
cook
self-service
feast
tablecloth
napkin
serviette
hamburger

sausage
soup
fish
tomato
potato
salt
pepper
sauce
meat
vegetable
dessert
pudding
trifle
jelly
custard
ice-cream
butter
cheese
salad
lettuce
cabbage

flavour
lemonade
coffee

reserved
juicy
tasty
appetizing
ravenous
impatient
tender
friendly
helpful
colourful
enjoyable
delicate

ordered
awaited
ate
tasted

Phrases

a special occasion
fruit juices
succulent roast chicken
a family outing
a large helping
a clean plate

healthy appetite
fish and chips
delicious aroma
three-course meal
hors d'oeuvre
chocolate mousse

Which is it?

Write each word adding the missing letters.
Use your dictionary if necessary.

Round 1   or or er?

groc___   settl___   seni__
auth___   lodg___   radiat___
charact___   maj___   hum___ous
doct___   equat___   vig___ous
sciss___s   instruct___   mot__
passeng___   conquer___   explor___

Round 2   ce or se?

inten___   presen___   nonsen___
___ntral   scien___   commen___
pen___   immen___   conden___
silen___   expen___   eviden___
senten___   differen___   suspen___
den___   justi___   absen___

Round 3   ant or ent?

vac_____   contin_____   pavem_____
excell_____   complim_____   contest_____
ignor_____   fragr_____   urg_____
assist_____   pleas_____   ornam_____
obedi_____   torr_____   presid_____
pati_____   confid_____   perman_____
extravag_____   accid_____   viol_____
emigr_____   anci_____   evid_____

Round 4   le or el?

chap____   artic____   sing____
puzz____   trav____   rif____
exc____   strugg____   thimb____
trif____   laur____   obstac____
mirac____   lab____   spectac____
lev____   squirr____   quarr____

Round 5   ie or ei?

gr___f   consc____nce   c____ling
v___l   n____ther   pat____nce
h___r   for____gn   misch____f
n___ce   l____sure   s____ze
bel___ve   suffic____nt   rel___f
handkerch____f n____ghbour   rec____ve

Round 6   able or ible?

vis_____   cap_____   suit_____
prob_____   sens_____   miser_____
imposs_____   veget_____   fashion_____
li_____   honour_____   invis_____
ed_____   respect_____   respons_____
horr_____   aud_____   reason_____

Round 7   l or ll?

sa__ute   exce__   exce__ent
vi__ain   woo__en   concea__ing
fu__fi__   wi__fu__   i__ustrate
annua__   we__come   compe__ed
a__together   trave__   jewe__ery

53

Word game—rule one

Adding -ed   -ing   -er   -ion

Look at these words:

admit	admitted	admitting
travel	travelling	traveller
rebel	rebelled	rebellion

The first word in each set ends in a vowel and a consonant. What happens when you add an ending beginning with a vowel?

Rule—longer words ending in a vowel and a consonant often double the last consonant when adding an ending beginning with a vowel.

Round 1	Add -ing to these words:	
begin	compel	commit
omit	expel	admit
parcel	regret	quarrel

Round 2	Add -ed to these words:	
quarrel	compel	occur
expel	omit	marvel
cancel	admit	permit
travel	level	prefer
regret	refer	commit

Round 3	Add -er to these words:	
begin	signal	travel
worship	jewel	propel

Word game—rule two

Compare the words in the two lists.

gallon	gale
tunnel	tune
current	cure

Notice that the words in the first list have
> two vowel sounds (two syllables)
> a double consonant
> a short initial vowel sound

Notice that the words in the second list have
> a single vowel sound (one syllable)
> single consonants
> a long initial vowel sound

Rule—a word of two syllables, where the initial vowel sound is short, often has a double consonant in the middle. Where the initial vowel sound is long it is often followed by a single consonant.

Spot the word that breaks the rule.

Round 1

rabbit	valley	common	miser
mirror	rotten	ruler	chapel

Round 2

channel	ivy	carrot	obey
tunnel	vessel	peril	Scottish

Round 3

differ	goddess	demon	diver
abbot	pillar	support	roller

Prefixes

Write one sentence to bring out the meaning of each word

Round 1   un- = not, without

unpaid	unfair	unaware
untrue	unhappy	unexplored
unjust	unheard	untouched
unemployed	unattractive	unfurnished

Round 2   dis- = not, the reverse of

disagree	disbelieve	disorder
discount	discover	disabled
disgrace	disappear	dishonest

Round 3   in- (or im-, il-, ir-, ig-) = not

infirm	innocent	injustice
incapable	illegal	irregular
incorrect	illegible	irresolute
ignoble	improbable	immature

Round 4   de- = down, from, away

descend	degrade	denote
depart	detail	depress
describe	despise	decrease
decay	deceive	deduce

Round 5   mis- = amiss, badly, wrongly

misplace	misguide	misjudge
mistrust	misfire	misname
mislead	misfortune	mistake

Round 6   ex- = out of, beyond, out

export	expect	expand
extract	exceed	excel
except	exclude	exclaim
exhale	expel	extra

Round 7   re- = back, again

recount	recollect	reflect
rebuild	readdress	report
return	repay	refloat
reinforce	refresh	relate

Round 8   trans- = across, beyond

transplant	transfer	transfuse
transmit	transport	transatlantic
translate	transparent	transpose
transcend	transit	translucent

Round 9   pro- = forth, for, forward, out

proceed	promote	propel
progress	protrude	produce
procession	pronoun	prophet
proclaim	prolong	project

Round 10   pre- = before

prefix	predict	preface
precede	precaution	prevent
preview	prefect	predominant
preclude	preconceive	predecessor

Round 11   tele- = far

television	telegraph	telescope
telephone	telegram	teleprinter

Suffixes

Write one sentence to bring out the meaning of each word.

Round 1   -ful = having much of, full

beautiful	faithful	useful
skilful	thoughtful	careful
plentiful	graceful	wonderful

Round 2   -less = free from, without

timeless	weightless	sightless
thoughtless	careless	homeless
useless	fearless	hopeless

Round 3   -able, -ible = capable of being

movable	admirable	likeable
edible	traceable	navigable
visible	respectable	audible
acceptable	habitable	inflammable
digestible	flexible	legible

Round 4   -let, -et, -ette = small

| cabinet | casket | locket |
| pamphlet | cigarette | leaflet |

Round 5   -er, -or = the person who

traveller	glazier	engineer
sailor	actor	doctor
labourer	conqueror	instructor

Round 6   -ous = full of

| famous | dangerous | humorous |

Useful things to know

Use a dictionary to find the meaning of the following words and phrases. Make up a sentence for each one.

Round 1

white elephant	by-pass	out-patient
the Ashes	satellite	post-mortem
neon sign	tournament	cul-de-sac

Round 2

suburb	monopoly	anthology
borough	barometer	spirit-level
manuscript	the Mint	paperback

Round 3

gross weight	wholesale	plumb-line
net weight	anecdote	fly-over
retail	terminus	bottle-neck

Round 4

barbecue	piebald	compasses
amphibian	coaster	ombudsman
locum	inventory	sonic boom
aviary	unique	municipal

Round 5

starboard	orienteering	generator
banquet	metropolis	bank holiday
smallholding	stop-press	pasteurized

Guess what?

Describe each of the following so that the object can be easily identified from your description.

a penny
a watch
a butterfly
an orange
a television set

a giraffe
ice-cream
a postage stamp
traffic lights
a magnet

a ruler
a sausage
a cloud
an umbrella
a snowflake

a torch
a robin.
a mouse
a piano
a pair of scissors

Say how!

Give instructions on how to:
clean your teeth
travel from your home to school
look after your pet
make a pot of tea
play your favourite game
sew on a button
plant and care for a flower bulb
lay the table for breakfast

What do you think?

Give your opinion for or against with reasons.

All pupils should wear school uniform.
Children under 14 should be in bed by 9 p.m.
All boys should learn to sew.
Girls should play football.
Television is a bad influence.
There are too many cars on the roads.

Insects

gnat	earwig	mosquito
centipede	beetle	daddy-long-legs
millipede	cockroach	butterfly

Trees

sycamore	beech	chestnut
hawthorn	rowan	willow
larch	yew	birch
spruce	monkey-puzzle	sequoia

Being ill

tonsilitis	headache	sickness
measles	appendicitis	influenza
chickenpox	diarrhoea	toothache
temperature	fever	medicine
prescription	disease	penicillin
convalescence	recovery	infection

First aid

bandage
poison
bruise
abrasion
accident
treatment
casualty

ointment
massage
sprain
disinfectant
strain
stretcher
examination

plaster
sterilize
scald
wound
patient
stitches
X-ray

Travel

coach
reservation
passport
tour
taxi
aeroplane
traveller

ferry
transport
luggage
souvenir
sightseeing
cruise
carriage

hovercraft
passenger
accommodation
excursion
customs
locomotive
station

Geography

equator
prairie
channel
estuary
ocean
cotton
coffee
steel
temperate
industry
export

tundra
harbour
plateau
hurricane
tobacco
vegetation
monsoon
region
chemicals
import
tourism

peninsula
tributary
Mediterranean
rubber
ore
resources
delta
coast
pampas
atoll
desert

The parts of speech

Three little words you often see
Are the **articles a, an** and **the**.

A **noun** is the name of anything
As **school** or **garden, ball** and **swing**.

Instead of nouns the **pronouns** play
As **I, thou, he, we, you** and **they**.

Adjectives tell the kind of noun
As **great, small, pretty, white** or **brown**.

Verbs tell of something to be done
To **read, count, sing, jump** or **run**.

How things are done the **adverbs** tell
As **slowly, quickly, ill** or **well**.

A **preposition** stands before a noun
As **in** or **through** the town.

An **interjection** shows surprise
As **Oh!** how pretty, **Ah!** how wise.

Conjunctions join the words together
Men **and** women, wind **or** weather.

The whole are called the nine **parts of speech**
Which reading, writing, speaking teach.

Science

oxygen
hydrogen
contraction
conduction
molecule
energy
litmus
vacuum
voltage
pressure
diagram

evaporation
magnetism
expansion
convection
radiation
motion
mass
thermometer
lever
gases
experiment

microscope
pendulum
crystal
balance
conductor
friction
velocity
temperature
mercury
magnetize
dissolve

Mathematics

square
parallel
pentagon
volume
vertex
bisect
decimal
probability

triangle
parallelogram
quadrilateral
cuboid
vertices
quotient
currency
difference

rectangle
rhombus
perimeter
area
equivalent
remainder
fraction
sequence

Regions of Britain

Somerset
Lincolnshire
Suffolk
Warwickshire
Strathclyde
Tayside
Londonderry

Leicestershire
Surrey
Lancashire
Norfolk
Grampian
Antrim
Gwent

Avon
Essex
Gloucestershire
Cumbria
Lothian
Armagh
Powys